# GOD'S
# PRESENCE
### *in the* LOSS *of a* CHILD

Bill Sanford's tender account of the turmoil and eventual loss of their precious newborn daughter, Stephanie, is a story filled with love and hope, despite the deep confusion and sorrow they experienced. The basis for this hope? God's grace, and God's grace alone. Here's a story that magnifies God in showing him to be the only adequate source of comfort, strength, hope and faith in a time of deep human loss. Praise be to God that no trial is too great for God's wisdom and strength, and no sorrow too deep that his love and care cannot penetrate. As Bill says over and again, because God is in control and God is good, we can know his wise purposes are being accomplished even through the trials and losses of life. Here is true hope, indeed.

—**Bruce A. Ware**, Professor of Christian Theology,
The Southern Baptist Theological Seminary

*God's Presence in the Loss of a Child*, is an account of a remarkable child and a grieving father. In this moving book, Bill Sanford reveals the heart of a grieving father and the hope of the gospel of Jesus Christ. This is the testimony of a believer, tested by fire, and a tribute to the sanctity of human life and the power of Christ in the midst of unspeakable loss.

—**R. Albert Mohler Jr.**, President
Southern Baptist Theological Seminary,
J.T. English Director of Theological Research,
Office of the President

This is a hard book to read, especially for a parent. In this personal testimony we hear from Bill and Melanie Sanford about what it means to lose a child. But, more than that, we hear their witness as to how God is faithful to his children.

—**Russell D. Moore**, President Ethics & Religious Liberty Commission, Southern Baptist Convention

Bill Sanford is an incredible Christian man with an incredible Christian story to tell. This book, *God's Presence in the Loss of a Child*, is straight from his heart to the reader's heart. It will prove to be encouraging reading for all, especially those who are grieving the loss of a loved one or are seeking to minister to someone who has.

—**Jason K. Allen**, Ph.D., President Midwestern Baptist Theological Seminary & College

This story of the death of Stephanie Sanford at twelve days old is told with as much tenderness and gentleness as the parents' all too short embrace of this child must have been. This is not only a riveting story, told with clarity and emotional immediacy, but is a lesson in how divine Providence, the secret operations of sustaining grace, and the liveliness of the word of God sustained Bill and Melanie Sanford and an entire church family in a twelve day life-or-death drama that Bill describes so graphically in the image of a roller coaster. God's glory shines through in Bill's pointing to Scripture and to the glory of Christ and the goodness of God interleaved through every moment of the quickly shifting scenes from hope to unknowing. We learn from this that all gifts are from God and he only takes from us that which he himself already has given. Our sense of loss is only possible because it was preceded by a sense of the overwhelming goodness of God in the bestowal of blessings. This book is a faithful testimony from a parent that has clearly been the object of tender mercies. It will be a great encouragement to many.

—**Tom J. Nettles**, The Southern Baptist Theological Seminary

There is nothing more difficult as a Pastor than ministering to a family who has lost a child. This book is a heart-felt declaration of the power of God through such a loss. These pages mirror the hearts of two parents finding hope in the midst of tragedy. A treasured piece for anyone searching for a glimmer of hope in the valley of the shadow of death.

—**Greg Payton**, Lead Pastor, The Rock Church, Laurel MT

*God's Presence in the Loss of a Child* brings purpose and focus to parents who are facing indescribable tragedy. This book is a marvelous tool for Pastors and church leaders who lead families from despair, grief, and sorrow to hope, purpose, and comfort.

—**Darwin Payton**, Director of Missions,
Yellowstone Southern Baptist Association.

I have known Bill Sanford for over ten years and he is a man that I greatly respect. Simply put, Bill is a man who walks with God and desires to make Him famous. I have seen God use Bill and his story to impact the lives of students and families through the years and I know that lives will continue to be impacted through this book.

—**Ben Trueblood**, Director of Student Ministry
at LifeWay of Christian Resources

To know Bill Sanford is to know a servant. His passion for the things of God and for others is evident in every manner of his life. On display in his book, we are given a insider's glimpse at the emotional, physical, and spiritual toll upon a family after the death of a baby girl. With great humility, Bill writes how Christ and the Church brought incredible healing and hope. This book is for everyone—those who have experienced the loss of a child and those who want to know how to encourage them.

—**Will Smallwood**, Vice President for University
Advancement, Oklahoma Baptist University

# GOD'S
# PRESENCE
### *in the* LOSS *of a* CHILD

Finding Hope, Purpose and Comfort
after the Death of a Loved One

## BILL SANFORD

NEW YORK

## GOD'S PRESENCE IN THE LOSS OF A CHILD

Finding Hope, Purpose and Comfort after the Death of a Loved One

ISBN 978-1-61448-775-3  paperback
ISBN 978-1-61448-776-0  eBook
Library of Congress Control Number: 2013941514

Morgan James Publishing
The Entrepreneurial Publisher
5 Penn Plaza, 23rd Floor,
New York City, New York 10001
(212) 655-5470 office • (516) 908-4496 fax
www.MorganJamesPublishing.com

**Cover Design by:**
Rachel Lopez
www.r2cdesign.com

**Interior Design by:**
Bonnie Bushman
bonnie@caboodlegraphics.com

In an effort to support local communities, raise awareness and funds, Morgan James Publishing donates a percentage of all book sales for the life of each book to Habitat for Humanity Peninsula and Greater Williamsburg.

Get involved today, visit
www.MorganJamesBuilds.com.

Habitat
for Humanity®
Peninsula and
Greater Williamsburg
Building Partner

The following pages reflect upon, are dedicated to, and are in memory of Stephanie Louise Sanford.

Noted are daily accounts of her brief but God-inspired life. Also mentioned are many instances that illustrate just how awesome and powerful God the Father really is, and that through His Son Jesus Christ you can find joy and peace even in the loss of a child.

It is still amazing even today, twenty-four years later, how God continues to put people in our lives who bless us and lift us up and remind us of His goodness and grace that He gave us several years ago.

God was so good to send His grace and mercy and extend His gentle hand of comfort to us. Whether it was a phone call, a card, or just a kind word from a friend, it was exactly what we needed to hear or read at that particular time.

We will never forget just how much Stephanie meant to us and the impact she had on my wife and me, as well as the lives of the other members of our family, our church family, our friends, our relatives, the hospital attendants, and many, many others— the ripples of which, while on this earth, we may never know.

# CONTENTS

# FOREWORD

The phone rang around 2:45 a.m., and I knew immediately that it was an emergency. I had been awakened earlier by a sense of urgency to pray, and I didn't even know for whom. When I heard Bill's voice I braced for bad news. "Melanie had a little girl, and they think there is a problem with her heart," he said. "Just pray." Hanging up the phone, I began to pray, "God, please let her live! For Bill and Melanie, please, God, let her live!"

I conveyed the news to my wife, Jeanie, and we quickly dressed and headed to the hospital. The horrible possibility of the death of a child at the climax of what was supposed to be such a joyous time dominated our thoughts on the way. We had been waiting for the Lord to give us a child for many years, and to think about Bill and Melanie in this situation left us in empathetic anguish.

I have never experienced a more difficult time in my life emotionally. Even when my own father died, the emotional stress was not as difficult to deal with. Baby Stephanie's life was brief, but she taught all of us so much about God's love and tender care. Probably more than I could ever teach in a lifetime of ministry.

Over a year ago, Bill asked me to write the introduction to Stephanie's story. Each time I started, I found it too painful to go on. It brought back the memories and emotions from more than fourteen years ago and made it feel like it was yesterday. I have found it impossible to write about Stephanie without tears flowing faster than my words. I am embarrassed that it has taken so long, but it has just been too incredibly painful for me to complete until now.

Today I was led to finish this request. Today the strength was given me to compose these inadequate words, encouraging you to read about a little girl named Stephanie. I am impressed to tell you that within this fragile struggle we call living, the death of a loved one has its purposes. Stephanie's story will bless you and help you and lead to your own healing if you have suffered the loss of a child.

You may be just at the beginning of the healing process. Nothing will ever take away the pain that you now bear, but there is hope for learning to live with your grief.

Bill and Melanie and I have already prayed for you, asking Jesus to give you strength, comfort, hope, and the help you need in living with the reality that your precious child is in His care. May you be encouraged, helped, and blessed by Stephanie's story.

Sincerely,

**Russ Robbins**

Minister of Education

First Baptist Church – Eufaula, AL

*Prologue*

# THE ROLLER COASTER RIDE

I really enjoy going to theme parks and riding all the different types of roller coasters. Imagine with me, for a moment, just how wild these rides can be. The lines always seem too long to wait in, but you step to the back of the line anyway and slowly move closer and closer to the front. Your heart starts beating faster and faster as "the moment" approaches. You watch as others get out of the cars, and you can see from the expressions on their faces that they have experienced the wildest ride of their lives.

You notice, as they step out, that not all of the passengers are smiling and laughing; some appear frightened and some are even crying. You hear others say that they never want to ride on a roller coaster again.

Two more groups of cars have left and returned. You are now at the front of the long line that you almost didn't even get in, and you're beginning to wonder if you really do want to ride or not. The attendant points to you. It is finally your turn, and you are seated in the car and strapped in for the ride.

The cars slowly leave the station, and you feel a slight jerk as you begin the slow pull up the high slope. The adrenaline starts pumping, and you become more and more anxious as you approach what seems to be the top of the world. Then the cars slowly creep over the peak, and for a brief moment it seems as if life has stopped. Immediately, you drop downward at a very fast and furious pace.

You finally reach the bottom of that first drop and are quickly driven into curves and turns and hoops as the coaster whisks along the tracks. From time to time it seems as though you are not even sitting in the seat, but just floating along.

And then, all of a sudden, the cars come to a stop as you reach the end of the ride. It all happened so fast. It didn't seem possible that the ride could have lasted only a few minutes.

What you are about to read is the story of the roller coaster ride that my wife, Melanie, and I were on for twelve days. Twelve days of our lives that at the time and through our eyes seemed to last forever. When it was over, it seemed to have been but the blink of an eye. Twelve days when at times our lives seemed turned upside down, only for us to soon find them level off in the peace of God. Twelve days when at times our lives seemed to have come to a stop, while at other times we just floated along as if in a dream. Twelve days that in many ways were like the very same three- to four-minute roller coaster ride. Twelve days leading up to God's glory.

As we go through our lives, no doubt many things will happen which we can't imagine God using for our good. God, in His sovereign and infinite wisdom, knows exactly what lies ahead in my life and in yours. We had to trust in Him and believe that He was in total control of our daughter's life. We had to believe that through her death He would be glorified and His kingdom would be lifted up and increased through the sharing of the story of her brief life.

So I would like to share with you some of the emotions that we experienced. Like a real roller coaster ride, there were many ups and downs and quick changes in direction. But through it all God never left our side. It is only through God and the grace of His Son Jesus Christ that we were able to have the strength to deal with our situation. He is the only one who deserves the honor and glory and praise.

# STEPHANIE'S STORY

Our roller coaster story began back in June of 1989. My wife Melanie, our two-and-a-half year-old son Trey, and I were living in a small, split-level house in a suburban town just south of Birmingham, Alabama. Melanie was nine months pregnant and our second child was due any day now. There had been no problems at all with my wife's pregnancy; all of her tests and sonograms had been perfectly normal. We had decided at an earlier date that we did not want to know whether the baby was a boy or a girl. Like most parents, we felt that really didn't matter as long as the baby was healthy.

We were very active members of a Baptist church about five minutes from where we lived, and I had just recently returned from a mission trip to Brazil. Even work was going very well. Life was just as it should be.

So, with all that said, let me try to tell you what has now become one of the most beautiful stories that I have been a part of thus far in my lifetime.

## Wednesday, June 14

All afternoon Melanie had the feeling that tonight was going to be the night. It was about 6 p.m. when she began having her first contractions. We spent the evening sitting around watching television. Her contractions started getting closer and closer together.

Around 9 p.m. we decided that we should probably start getting things in order to go to the hospital.

Trey was already asleep. I called Melanie's sister to see if she would come over and stay with him for the night while we were at the hospital.

We arrived at the hospital around 10:30 p.m. After a brief examination by the doctor, the decision was made to go ahead and admit Melanie to a room. Everything was going just perfect. It was very evident that during the next few hours we were going to have a baby.

## Thursday, June 15

Other than the typical birth pains that Melanie experienced, the next four hours went pretty well. At exactly 2:36 a.m. our little girl was born. We named her Stephanie Louise Sanford.

She was beautiful. She looked as healthy and normal as any baby could look at that moment. She weighed seven pounds and three ounces and was twenty inches long.

I made the statement, "Everything must be OK. She has ten little fingers and ten little toes."

The nurse took Stephanie from the doctor, wrapped her in a blanket, and handed her to Melanie. We both were extremely excited and proud to have a little girl. We still thought that everything was physically all right.

Within the first two to three minutes after her arrival, we noticed that Stephanie was having some difficulty breathing. Her color was changing to blue. We began to notice she did not cry as loudly or as much as she probably should have.

And then, all of a sudden, within an instant, the nurses were taking Stephanie from Melanie and giving her oxygen. After a few minutes the nurses took Stephanie from our room to an area down the hallway where other newborn babies were. There was more technical equipment on hand to help Stephanie with her breathing. At least five or six nurses and a doctor surrounded Stephanie's little bed. They were so close to one another that I could not even see her.

It was at that moment that I began to get very nervous. What if something was indeed wrong with our child? How could this be happening to us? Everything had seemed to go just as it was supposed to. Was this really happening, or was it just a bad dream?

I knew that I needed to call someone from our church. Russ Robbins was our minister of education. He and his wife, Jeannie, joined the church on the same day Melanie and I did back in August of 1985. They had grown to be wonderful and close friends of ours.

It was a little before three o'clock in the morning. I called Russ and told him that there were some problems with Stephanie's breathing, and that we did not know how serious it might be. I found out later on in the week that Russ had been awakened around 2 a.m. and felt the need to pray for someone in the church. You see, even prior to Stephanie being born and before she would be in the hands of the doctors, God had already taken matters into His own hands.

We had parents and other family members at the hospital. I was going back and forth from Melanie's room to the nursery to the waiting room, trying as best I could to keep everyone informed. One minute I was checking on my wife and the next minute I was checking on my daughter and the next minute I was trying to tell our family members what was going on. All the while, I struggled to remain as strong and under control as I possibly could.

After about an hour, one of the head nurses stopped me in the hall between Melanie's room and Stephanie's room. She looked me straight in the eye and said, "You've got a sick little girl here, Daddy." I can't tell you how hard those words hit me. It was at that moment I realized that Stephanie was not all right, as I had thought only an hour or so ago. It had happened that fast.

The doctors at this hospital were not sure exactly what was wrong with Stephanie or what they could do for her. Arrangements were made for her to be transported to another hospital that was better equipped to assess and care for babies with her condition. A cardiologist was scheduled to meet Stephanie and the transport team once they arrived.

Stephanie's transport team and I arrived at St. Vincent's Hospital shortly after 5 a.m. It had only been two and a half hours since Stephanie was born. We went straight up to the Neonatal Intensive Care Unit (NICU) where a team of doctors and nurses were quickly attending to Stephanie, desperately trying to assess her problem with breathing.

About an hour and a half later, the cardiologist and one other doctor came into the small waiting room where I was to tell me what they had found wrong with my little girl.

My parents were with me, along with our dear friends from church, Russ and Jeannie Robbins. I took a very deep breath as the doctor began to speak. What he had to say was not good at all. In fact he said exactly what the nurse at the other hospital had told me earlier: "You've got a very sick little girl here, Daddy."

Stephanie had problems with both her heart and one of her lungs. The doctors gave me no quick guarantees that in due time she would be OK; they did say they would do the very best they possibly could, but that there was only so much they as doctors could do with the seriousness of her illness.

At first I began to wonder what it was that I had done to deserve this. Why was God punishing Stephanie for something I had done? I was confused as to how to pray and just what to pray for. Was I to pray for Stephanie's complete healing or for God to just go ahead and take her now if she was not going to be able to live a good and prosperous life? My mind seemed to be running away from me with all these thoughts and doubts and worries.

What happened next probably is what saved me from having a breakdown.

Russ saw me pacing back and forth and up and down the hallway. He walked up to me and grabbed me by the arm firmly. We walked down the hall away from everyone to a quiet room. He told me not to speak but to just sit and listen for a while. One verse of Scripture that he shared with me was Proverbs 3:5. It read, "Trust in the LORD with all your heart and lean not on your own understanding."

You see, God is always in control of the things that go on in our lives, even when sometimes we may not be. After several minutes of talking about our situation, the circumstances, and the options, Russ prayed for me. He prayed for Stephanie to be completely healed. He prayed for strength and for a peace of mind for Melanie and me. I now knew the direction in which to go. This was going to be way too big for me to handle; I had to give it all to God. Not part of our situation, but all of it!

Within an instant I felt much more at ease. I knew beyond a shadow of a doubt that God was in complete control and that I was going to trust Him totally with whatever the results turned out to be.

I went back to the hospital where Melanie was about 8 a.m. to check on her and tell her what the doctors had said about Stephanie's condition. We spent a few minutes alone, sometimes talking and sometimes crying, until we were able to regain a little composure. We were both upset and unsure about what was going to happen, but we knew we needed to let several of our friends know what was going on. We needed everyone to be lifting us up in prayer and praying for Stephanie's condition as well.

We were still in Melanie's room making phone calls around 9 a.m. Melanie's sister Sherry had brought our son, Trey, into the room. A few days prior to coming to the hospital, we had bought Trey a gift that was to be from Stephanie. We did not count on these circumstances in which to give him the present. Melanie and I both had a really tough time telling him what was going on with his little sister, Stephanie, and giving him the present she had for him. Trey was only two, and it was not possible for him to understand what was happening to his baby sister.

Knowing that we still had Trey gave Melanie and me a feeling of relief, joy, and peace.

God was indeed answering our prayers, and we knew that He would see us through this.

Around ten that morning, Melanie was discharged from the hospital so that she could go across town to be with Stephanie. Remember, we had arrived at the hospital only eleven and a half hours earlier. Melanie had given birth to Stephanie only seven and a half hours ago, and now the doctors were releasing her under our own care and responsibility.

Later that day as we reflected back we realized that God had orchestrated Melanie's release from the hospital. For her to be both physically and emotionally able to leave as soon as she did was unbelievable.

When we arrived at the hospital where Stephanie was, already several of our friends were waiting to see us. During the next three or four hours many friends kept coming and going. Melanie and I noticed that the Lord was giving us a peace about Stephanie's condition and that everything was going to be all right, no matter what. We knew that many people were praying for us. Our emotional and physical strength and our peace of mind were an answer to all those prayers.

By late afternoon, Stephanie had been in the NICU for about ten hours and the nurses had her condition stabilized.

We were given a room right down the hall from the NICU. Melanie and I seemed to go back and forth all day long checking on her.

It was about 6 p.m. when I asked Melanie how she felt about staying at the hospital that night. She and I agreed that it would be a good idea. We made arrangements for Trey to be taken care of that night while we stayed at the hospital with Stephanie.

We continued to go in and check on Stephanie as well as visit with many of our friends who had come up later in the day. This went on for a few more hours and then it seemed as though we both just ran out of steam at the same time. We decided to say thank you and goodnight to our friends and go back to our room to get a little sleep.

This no doubt had been one of the longest days of our lives.

**Friday, June 16**
Melanie and I woke up early in the morning anxious to see Stephanie. The NICU nurses came in to tell us that she had done pretty well all night long and that her condition was still listed as stable.

It was very difficult for us to realize just how sick Stephanie really was. She was a full-term, eight-pound beautiful little baby girl. Melanie had not experienced any difficulty in the past nine months of her pregnancy. It just didn't seem possible that Stephanie could be as sick as the doctors said she was. We weren't blaming God for this, and we did not feel that God had purposely done this to her, but we did not understand.

The reality of all this was setting in, that this was really happening to us. This was not just a bad dream. We did not know how long this might go on or even whether or not Stephanie would live.

Later that night our emotions began catching up with us. By no means were we starting to lose hope. We were wearing down a little and were still not quite sure how to adjust to something like this. We started wondering things like: What's going to happen to Stephanie? How are we to act? What are we to say to our friends? When are we to pray, and what are we to pray for? What is it that God wants us to learn from this? How much longer is this going to go on, and will we be strong enough, both emotionally and spiritually, regardless of what happens?

Sometimes in life we go through things that test our faith. Will we be able to separate our faith from the reality? Will we pray for others to be strong when they endure hardships and then, when it is our time to pass through the fire, just give up? Or will we be strong in our faith, trust in God, and allow Him to use us as witnesses unto others through our actions? God wants all of us to see the good in our trials, but in order for Him to do this we must be able to turn the entire circumstance over to Him, not just part of it.

Around 8:30 p.m., a couple of families from our church came by to visit. They brought us cards and some small pieces of literature. One of the cards had a verse on it that seemed the most perfect verse for us at that time. It was Jeremiah 29:11: "For I know the plans I have for you, declares the Lord. Plans to prosper you and not to harm you. Plans to give you a hope and a future."

My brother, Charles, took a marker and wrote this passage in big, bold letters on a piece of poster board, along with Stephanie's name, and taped it on the wall in our hospital room. This was a visible reminder that God was, and always had been, in complete control of this very real walk in our life.

## Saturday and Sunday, June 17–18

Melanie and I spent the whole weekend at the hospital, with family and friends by our side the entire two days. It was also really good to be able to spend a lot of time with Trey. Several times each day, Trey and I would walk to the NICU together. I would pick him up in my arms and we would look through the window at his little sister and Daddy's little girl. Trey was only a toddler, and like us he couldn't really understand just how sick Stephanie was, why she had to be in the hospital, and why we couldn't just take her home.

As time passed, we heard wonderful stories from friends about other friends, families, groups, and churches in other areas, cities, and even states that were praying for us. They were praying for us to have strength, for us to have peace of mind, for the full recovery of our daughter, and for us to be able to trust in God's will for our lives.

We both knew that it was through these prayers and by the grace of God that we were able to stay focused on where we were and on what might lie ahead.

Something we hadn't thought a lot about was that Melanie had delivered Stephanie just four days ago. Beginning as early as the first day, Thursday morning, God was giving her the strength physically, mentally, and especially emotionally to handle this situation. She never once had any type of after-birth problems or pains, nor did she experience any emotional breakdowns. We knew this was because of prayers being lifted up for her and by the grace of God Himself. There is no other answer.

Well, our little Stephanie was still hanging in there. Up to now she hadn't regressed any. At the same time, she was not showing much improvement either. Even so, it was still early and we continued to remain very optimistic because we knew beyond a shadow of a doubt that the Lord had His hand on Stephanie and that He was in complete control of this entire experience.

## Monday, June 19

Early that morning the doctors came to our room to let us know they had decided to transfer Stephanie to UAB Hospital in

Birmingham. The plan was to get her scheduled and prepared for surgery sometime during the week.

The NICU at UAB Hospital was very different from the one we just left. For one thing, it was very difficult to get to—located right in the middle of downtown Birmingham. The atmosphere there seemed more hectic and businesslike. There was only one very small waiting room on the fifth floor where the NICU was located.

During this time, that particular NICU was taking care of twice the number of babies as they were set up to care for. You can only imagine how all this created more confusion for us.

Everything went smoothly during Stephanie's transport. By late that afternoon she was settled in her bed and her condition was again stabilized. There were so many tubes and wires hooked up to her that she needed to remain as still as possible, so the doctors kept her sedated and asleep much of the time.

About 6 p.m. we decided to go down to the cafeteria on the second floor to sit around and wait awhile. Here, there was much more room for all of our family and friends to talk and visit.

A little later on that night, after most of our friends had left, Melanie and I were wondering what we should do and whether we should spend the night at the hospital. Stephanie's condition was stabilized, and the only place to stay over would be the waiting room.

Here at UAB we did not have the luxury of staying in our own room right down the hall as we did at the other hospital. Something else we had to consider was that we did have a young son waiting on us at home who still did not really understand what was going on or why we needed to spend so much time away from him.

So, after a little debating over this, we decided that where we were needed the most that night was at our own home with Trey. This was the first time since Stephanie was born, five days earlier, that we had left her side.

The Bible tells us that God knows our deepest thoughts and most painful hurts. He knew that we were really more tired and worn down than depressed. As we were walking out one of the doors of this very large hospital we ran into some of our friends from church. God had arranged our meeting perfectly. He knew that after a short visit with these two couples our spirits would be lifted up again.

On the drive home we talked about some of the specific ways that God had been with us through these past several days. We knew that God had intervened and sustained us by His grace in our current circumstances. Many of our own families' lives had already been touched in a special way by Stephanie's life, and they were now a little closer to God.

One scripture was beginning to stand out in both of our minds. It was Romans 8:28: "And we know that in all things

God works for the good of those who love the Lord and are called according to His purpose."

God was fulfilling His promise to us that He made in this scripture. We still did not know what the next days, weeks, or months would be like. For that matter we did not know what tomorrow morning would bring. What we did know was that no matter what happened, if we kept God first in everything we did and trusted in His will for our lives, He would sustain us and see us through this—and somehow something very positive was going to come from this and we would be able to give God the glory for all that He had done for us.

## Tuesday, June 20

Melanie and I got up very early to get ready to go to the hospital. After I showered, while Melanie finished getting herself ready, I sat down to read some Scripture. I pretty much just opened my Bible and there was Philippians 2:25–30. It was as if God Himself had turned the pages there. It reads:

> But I thought it necessary to send to you Epaphroditus, my brother and fellow worker and fellow soldier, who is also your messenger and minister to our need; because he was longing for you all and was distressed you had heard that he was sick. For indeed he was

sick to the point of death, but God had mercy on him, and not only him, but also on me, lest we should have sorrow upon sorrow. Therefore, I have sent him all the more eagerly in order that when you see him again, you may rejoice and I may be less concerned about you. Therefore, receive him in the Lord with all joy, and hold men like him in high regard; because he came close to death for the work of Christ, risking his life to complete what was deficient in your service to me.

Today the world seems to honor those who are intelligent, beautiful, rich, and powerful. If this is true, what kind of people does that leave for the church to honor and lift up? In these scriptures the apostle Paul is indicating that we should honor those who give their lives for the sake of Christ. They could be missionaries oversees or just our family members and friends who are there for us when we need them the most.

God will most definitely put us in places for ministry, but we must be willing to be used and be obedient to share the Good News of Christ with those He puts in our path. And sometimes all that is required is something as simple as just being around and close to those who are hurting, letting them know that we are there and are praying for them.

When we arrived at the hospital, about 7 a.m., the nurses told us that Stephanie was still maintaining her stable condition.

Some of our friends came up to see how things were going during the next few hours. We were in and out of the NICU many times, talking with the nurses to see if we could find out anything new. Later that morning we finally got the chance to talk to the doctors who were caring for Stephanie. They told us they had reviewed her condition and wanted to go ahead and schedule her for a cauterization test sometime that afternoon. This test would confirm exactly what the doctors suspected her problems were. They informed us that there was a fifty-fifty chance she might not survive the procedure.

This was the first time we were facing a situation that separated faith and reality—the same type of situation in which we had prayed for others to be strong and courageous and to put their trust in God so that He might provide peace and grace in their lives. Now we were in the furnace, and it was time for us to put our faith and trust in God to the test.

What was especially tough was that we were approaching what might be the last time we saw our daughter alive.

It was already early afternoon. We had been so caught up in visiting with Stephanie, friends, nurses, and finally the doctors that we had not taken the time to get anything to eat. We went down to the cafeteria with a few of our friends and family members to wait until it was time for Stephanie's procedure.

The next several hours passed by ever so slowly. We finally got a call about 4:30 p.m. to come back up to the NICU. We watched as the nurses prepared Stephanie to move to another area of the hospital. She still had to remain sedated. There were many tubes and wires and monitors that had to be swapped around from stretcher to stretcher. The nurses that work in these units are very special people in their own way. They were all so good with Stephanie and took tremendous care of her.

Melanie was sitting in a rocking chair right next to Stephanie's bed, and I was standing behind her. We were both so quiet and still as they cared for her. It just did not seem possible, or fair, that our little girl who was born full-term should be so ill. If you looked past the tubes, she seemed so perfect.

Even with all that had gone on up to this point, we still knew that God had not intentionally done this to us and that He was in complete control of our situation. He "allows" these kinds of events to exist because of our sins that go all the way back to Adam and Eve and the fall of man as we read in Genesis 3.

What we as Christians must do when we are faced with trials and tribulations in our lives is to stay focused on the cross and the price that our Lord and Savior Jesus Christ paid for us so that we might have life everlasting. We also must understand that Jesus has been through much more than we ever will. Scripture tells us that God will not put more on us than we are spiritually capable of handling.

It came time for the nurses to move Stephanie to the other stretcher. We had to go out into the hall as the final preparations were made. Both of us, at the same time, as if it had been rehearsed, leaned over and kissed Stephanie. Then we just slowly backed up and out the door and into the hallway.

A few minutes later the nurses wheeled Stephanie out of the NICU room and into the hallway. There were a few family members and friends with us, and the nurses stopped the stretcher so we could speak to her once again.

All of a sudden, as we were looking at Stephanie, she opened her eyes for the first time and looked right at both of us. It was as if she was telling us that everything was going to be all right, that she would see us in a little while, and that we needed to remember what the prophet Jeremiah said—that God had a plan for her life, and He wasn't quite through with that plan yet.

As you can imagine, this was a very emotional and yet nervous time for both of us.

The doctors had told us the procedure would take about an hour to perform. During this time we were told we needed to remain in the surgery waiting room until they called for us.

Earlier in the day a friend had come to visit and brought us a card with a scripture on it. Once again God knew exactly what we needed at exactly the right time. The scripture could not have been any more uplifting. That most perfect Bible verse was Isaiah 41:10:

> Do not fear, for I am with you; do not anxiously look about you, for I am your God. I will strengthen you, surely I will help you, surely I will uphold you with my righteous right hand.

This verse was extremely comforting to us at this particular time. God knows exactly what the future holds. He will guide us through our times of trouble if we will only look to Him and rely on His strength and not our own. We are promised this from the prophet Isaiah. All believers are God's chosen people, and all share in the responsibility of presenting Him to the world. The day will come when God will bring all of His faithful people together. In the meantime, we have the assurance that He is able to help us get through the trials in our life.

Just as the doctors had said, we had been waiting about an hour when they came to tell us that Stephanie had done very well during the procedure. I can't tell you how relieved we all were.

A little later on, about 7:30 or 8 p.m., after the doctors had the chance to view the X-rays and get the results from their test on Stephanie, they came into our waiting room to tell us what they had seen. They told us that her condition, as bad as it was,

was just what they had expected. In other words, there were not any new surprises or complications that they would have to deal with during surgery.

Stephanie was still very ill with major heart and lung problems, but at least there were not any new hurdles for her to have to get over.

We spent a few more hours with Stephanie, watching the nurses stabilize her once again and visiting with family and friends. Later, being exhausted, we decided to go on home for the night and try to get a little sleep.

## Wednesday, June 21

We arrived at the hospital very early that morning in hopes of talking to the doctors sometime between 6:30 and 7:30 a.m., before they started making their rounds. I was more uptight and nervous than I had ever been up to this point. It was about 11 before we had the opportunity to speak with one of Stephanie's doctors. He said he had conferred with the other doctors and that they were going to go ahead and schedule her for surgery sometime that day. We were told that it could possibly be as late as 11 p.m. before they took her for surgery.

For some reason I was having a really difficult time dealing with things all of a sudden. It wasn't as if I had given up hope or stopped having faith, but I just didn't feel as if I was up to whatever the results of the day might present.

Around noon, five of my buddies showed up. The really miraculous thing is that they all showed up at exactly the same time. There was no way that this was a coincidence. UAB Hospital is a huge complex made up of several blocks of buildings, parking decks, crossover bridges, elevators, and who knows how many miles of hallways. For all five of these guys, coming from different places all over the city of Birmingham, to converge on me at the exact same time was nothing short of an act of God. There is no other possible answer.

My immediate words to them were, "Guys, will you all go down to the chapel and pray with me...now?" We left the second-floor cafeteria area and went down to the first floor where the chapel was so that we could all pray together.

As soon as the six of us began praying, I could tell that I was regaining some of the strength, confidence, and peace of mind that had seemed to slip away.

After fifteen or twenty minutes, I got up and thanked my friends for coming down to see me during their lunch break. I didn't know how well I would have made it through the day if they had not showed up. The power of prayer can be an amazing thing.

When we opened the chapel door, there in the doorway were two other very special friends of mine that I had known most of my life. We likewise went into the chapel to pray for a while.

God was continuing to place people with me that could lift me up in prayer. Sometimes we just don't realize how powerful and awesome our almighty God is. He always seems to be there for us. At the times in which we need Him the most, He has already begun putting people in our path and working miracles in our lives.

He had structured and timed everything perfectly for my five friends that morning, from the moment they got out of bed, went to work, left their offices, drove downtown to UAB Hospital, found a parking space, and walked into the hospital, to the *exact moment* that they met me in the hallway on the second floor, just in front of the cafeteria. There is no other possible answer than God Himself.

After about an hour or so, Melanie sent someone down to the chapel to get me. It was time for us to meet with Stephanie's surgeon, Dr. Kirkland. It was now about one o'clock in the afternoon.

Melanie and I met with the doctor alone in a small conference room down the hall from the NICU. He explained to us what the surgical options were for Stephanie. He said what she really needed was a heart and lung transplant, but that procedure had never been done before. The next option was to go ahead and repair her heart and lung at the same time. This procedure would give her only a 2 percent chance of surviving the operation. The third option was to repair her lung now and then at a later date, in two or three years, operate again and try to repair her heart. This particular procedure would leave her with only a 10-15 percent chance for living. As bleak as it might have seemed at the time, it appeared that this was our only option.

The doctor explained that the procedure would take a couple of hours once she was prepped and ready for surgery.

Just outside this little conference room, several of our family members and friends were waiting for us. We all watched through the glass window as the nurses prepared to move Stephanie to the surgical area.

A nurse came out into the hall and asked Melanie if she would like to come in and hold Stephanie for a moment before they took her to surgery. Prior to this, the only chance that Melanie had to hold Stephanie was just after giving birth, for only two or three minutes.

As we walked into the NICU, we both realized again that this might be the last time we saw our precious little daughter alive. I don't know if we were trembling more with fear or excitement.

The nurse gently placed Stephanie into Melanie's arms and we just quietly stared at our little girl, the many tubes and wires still connected to different parts of her body. With tears running down our faces, we told her how much we loved her and that everything was going to be all right.

After a few minutes, the nurse said it was time to make the final preparations for surgery. Melanie ever so slowly handed

Stephanie over to the nurse. We walked back into the hallway and watched through the window.

The nurses brought Stephanie out of the NICU and down the hallway. They briefly stopped in front of Melanie and me for us to speak to her before her surgery. Just as before, she briefly opened her eyes and looked straight up at the both of us. I felt like I was going to fall to my knees. Again, it was as though she was letting us know that she was in the hands of the Father and that everything was going to be OK. There are times in all our lives that we will always remember and hold very special. This no doubt was going to be one of those times.

The surgery waiting room at UAB is where we were supposed to go and wait during Stephanie's operation, just down the hall from the cafeteria on the second floor. We guessed that they began the operation around 2:30 that afternoon. Time seemed to creep.

Several more family members and friends came by to see how we were doing. There were as many as thirty-five of us in the waiting room and spilling out into the hall. It was such a comfort to us that there were so many people to pray for us and for Stephanie.

Finally, about 4:30 p.m., a phone call from Dr. Kirkland came in to us. The attendant stood up at the counter and called out my name over the intercom. There was a quiet hush around the waiting room as I stood up and moved toward the desk. I was wondering whether or not our daughter was OK or even if she was still alive. Shaking with fear, I took the phone from the attendant and slowly put it up to my ear.

"Hello, this is Bill Sanford," I said, and the first words I heard were "Mr. Sanford, your little girl has survived the operation. She is in stable but serious condition." This was the best news I had heard since the time of her birth. I turned and with tears in my eyes gave two thumbs up to my wife, who was standing in front of our family. Word quickly spread into the hallway where other relatives and friends had so very patiently been waiting. The entire room and hallway were filled with cheers, thanks, and praises to the Father, who is the Master Physician.

I have often wondered how I would have reacted, in front of all those other people, and what our life would have later been like if that phone call had delivered the devastating news that our little girl had not made it.

I am reminded of a Scripture passage, 2 Corinthians 4:6, which says, "For God, who commanded the light to shine out of darkness, hath shined in our hearts, to give the light of the knowledge of the glory of God in the face of Jesus Christ."

As we go through life, it is most certain that we will face difficulties. These trials can seem to paralyze us with fear if for one moment we take our eyes off the only one who can sustain us. Jesus tells us that if we will just keep our eyes on Him and take things one step at a time, He will faithfully lead us to the other side of our danger or difficulty by giving us the strength and wisdom that we need.

My prayer is that wherever my life leads me I will always stay focused on the one who not only created me but loved me enough to be crucified and die on a cross so that I might have life and one day spend the rest of eternity with Him in heaven. What a comfort that is for us.

After several more minutes of visiting with our friends and thanking them for coming to see us, we went back up to the floor where the NICU is located to wait for the nurses to bring Stephanie back. When they wheeled her bed by us, I can't tell you how we both felt. We were so glad to see her and thought that she looked so beautiful. The nurses carefully moved her onto her bed and began hooking the tubes and monitors back on her precious little body. I remember the two of us just standing there in silence, looking through the glass at our little girl. She had just been through so much, yet she looked at peace and well.

We remained at the hospital a few more hours, telling others of the wonderful news. It seemed as if God had planned someone to come to visit with us just as someone else was leaving. Not once were we ever left feeling alone and all by ourselves. We knew that God was with us every minute of every day and would see us through this time in our lives. We did not know if the outcome was going to be several days, weeks, months, or even years away, but we trusted in God to give us the peace and comfort and strength to handle whatever the situation might be.

### Thursday, June 22

We once again arrived at the hospital very early. As the shifts were changing, we overheard some of the attending doctors and nurses saying that they were amazed to see Stephanie back on the floor. I commented to them "that as good as Dr. Kirkland is as a surgeon, yesterday he had a little help with Stephanie from the Master Physician Himself." And the really neat thing was that they all agreed.

The doctors soon came by and talked to us about Stephanie. They reported they were "cautiously optimistic" about her condition. The plan was to go ahead and have her transported back to the previous hospital for what would probably be several weeks of recovery time. This was the most fantastic news we could have possibly heard. I mean think about it. Our little eight-pound, one-week-old baby girl undergoes major surgery and within twenty-four hours is being moved to another hospital for recovery.

We spent the rest of the morning and early part of the afternoon visiting with friends and calling others to tell them about the wonderful news that Stephanie was going back to St. Vincent's Hospital.

Stephanie left UAB Hospital with people cheering and waving as she pulled away in the ambulance. It was about three o'clock in the afternoon, and the drive to St. Vincent's would only take about ten minutes.

Everything about the transport went perfectly. She was resting in the NICU in no time. Melanie and I felt so much better about Stephanie being back at St. Vincent's Hospital. We were able to be closer to her and felt the atmosphere was a little less businesslike.

As was the case when Stephanie came back from her surgery at UAB, some of the nurses at St. Vincent's were surprised to see her back. They knew what her condition had been and were so glad to have the opportunity to care for her again. With all these good things happening so fast, it was not hard for us to feel optimistic about Stephanie's condition and her recovery.

## Friday, June 23

With all that had been happening the last few days, we found it hard to sleep at night. We were still sort of in a state of shock and amazement. We were not accustomed to times such as these which demanded our all.

As we were getting ready to go to the hospital, we both commented how strange and yet comforted we were feeling.

We were only four and a half years into our marriage, and we wondered if God was testing us and preparing us for things to come in our life down the road.

When we arrived at the NICU, we spoke with the nurse concerning how Stephanie had fared through the night. She told us that her condition had been improving just slightly every few hours throughout the night.

Even though we had come to terms with leaving Stephanie in the hospital for several more weeks, we were now feeling certain that we would be able to take our little girl home. We were going to make sure that she had a great life ahead of her.

Later in the day we went home to our son, Trey, feeling sky-high and telling him that in a few weeks we would be bringing his little baby sister home to live with us.

## Saturday, June 24

We got a call from the doctor early that morning as we were getting dressed and ready to go to the hospital. He told us that Stephanie had not had a very good night. Her condition had regressed over the past six to eight hours, and at the present time her condition was not good. This was surely a moment of rapid emotional change, something we were growing accustomed to since her birth.

We hurried to the hospital and up to the NICU. When the doctor saw us, he told us not to get our hopes up just yet and to be prepared for whatever might happen. This was the biggest setback that we'd had in a few days.

We began calling some of our family and friends to update them on how things were at the present time. Melanie remembered a Scripture passage that she had read earlier in the week. It was from Hebrews 10:35-39 and 11:1, and 6. We went down to the waiting room, got out our Bibles, and read these verses together.

Therefore, do not throw away your confidence, which was a great reward. For you have need of endurance, so that when you have done the will of God, you may receive what was promised. For yet in a very little while, he who is coming will come and will not delay. But My righteous one shall live by faith; and if he shrinks back, my soul has no pleasure in him. But we are not of those who shrink back to destruction, but of those who have faith to the preserving of the soul....

Now faith is the assurance of things hoped for, and the evidence of things not seen....And without faith it is impossible to please Him, for he who comes to God must believe that He exists and that He rewards those who earnestly seek Him.

The writer of Hebrews encourages us not to abandon our faith in times of trouble or persecution, but to show by our endurance that our faith is real. Faith means resting and believing in what Christ has done for us in the past, but it also means trusting in Him for what He is going to do for us today and in the future. You see, God does not just want us to know *about* Him. He wants us to have a very personal relationship *with* Him, one that will transform our lives.

Reading these verses gave us the boost we needed to get ourselves back together. The doctor said that if Stephanie's condition improved just a little during the course of the day, he would be pleased. Needless to say, we would be too.

By now it was about 9 a.m., and we both knew we needed to get on the phone and start letting everyone know what was going on and how much we needed their prayers. We knew that some of the people would also call someone else, and so on and so forth. In that way word of Stephanie's condition would spread quickly.

Within one hour Stephanie's monitors had begun showing some improvement. Is that the power of prayer or what?

She held her own for the rest of the day, and by that night, around 9 p.m., her condition was even slightly more improved. This was just what the doctor had said he wanted.

After the stressful day, and because it was already pretty late, we both decided to stay at the hospital that night. We felt like we wanted to be as close to Stephanie as possible in case she had another night like the one before.

## Sunday, June 25

Well, it was a new day, and to be quite honest, we did not know exactly what to expect when we went in to see how Stephanie was doing early that morning. We crept in to see her about 5:30 a.m., and it was just amazing. She looked great! The nurses had bathed her and put red ribbons on her right wrist and in her hair. We just knew that it was going to be a great day. As a matter of fact, Stephanie seemed to be doing so well, and her condition was so stabilized, that we decided to slip out of the hospital and go to Sunday school and church.

When we got to Sunday school, several of the classes gathered downstairs to speak to us and see how we were doing. I was asked to give a testimony as to what had been taking place in our lives over the last several days. As unprepared as we were to do this, and as difficult as it was to speak through our emotion, we both weathered the storm and told of our experiences. Nothing we said had to do with us at any time blaming God for what was happening. In fact, if it had not been for the grace of God, we would not have even been there. Yes, we were going through an extremely difficult time in our lives, but God had always been there, one step ahead of us, preparing the way.

After the service we spoke to as many people as we could and then headed back to the hospital. It was a quiet afternoon, with some of our family and relatives coming by to see us.

Stephanie was still kept in a sedated state. She still had so many monitors hooked up to her, but that didn't seem to matter to us at all. We were able to blot out those tubes and wires and just see a beautiful little girl who was loved as much as any baby girl could be.

My mother had put some pink socks on her tiny feet, and the nurse had changed her red ribbons to pink ones. You can imagine how pretty she looked. After all, that's how Daddy's little girl was supposed to look, wasn't it?

## Monday, June 26

We decided that we would try to get ourselves back into some kind of a routine this week. We had been told that Stephanie would be in the hospital for several weeks. I did have a job that I needed to get back to, and I thought today would be as good a day as any to try to get back to some amount of normalcy in our lives.

I arrived at the hospital at 5:30 a.m. A friend of mine from church was meeting me there for breakfast and some prayer time.

Stephanie's condition appeared to be just a little better than it was yesterday; however, her ventilator rate had not changed since Thursday night. The nurses were beginning to express a little concern about this. When we left, we committed to pray specifically for her ventilator rate to come down.

I went on to the office for a while but couldn't quite get back into the swing of things just yet. So, about noontime, I decided to go back up to the hospital. There was no change in her ventilator rate, but her condition in a couple of other areas was improving slightly. After an hour or so at the hospital, I left to go back to the office. I kept on praying for her ventilator rate to come down.

About 2:30 p.m., Melanie called me at the office. The nurses had moved Stephanie's ventilator down about five settings. Later on that afternoon when I got there, about 4:30 p.m., it was down another five settings.

Once again we were both feeling very optimistic about getting to take our little girl home in three or four weeks.

Early that evening the doctor came to tell us the results of the brain scan that was done on the previous day. They said that everything was normal and that all of Stephanie's other organs were normal and looking good also. So, after a little consultation time with the doctors, a decision was made as to what they were going to do and which direction was the best for Stephanie.

What the doctors said they would like to do would be to bring Stephanie back in two or three years, when she was strong enough, to have heart surgery. They went on to tell us that there was no reason after that that she would not be able to go on and live a normal life.

When we went home that night, we were feeling about as proud and hopeful as we had thus far. It appeared as though before long Stephanie would be home with her family, living out her life as God had intended. At least we were hoping and praying that was God's intention for her.

## Tuesday, June 27

Early that morning three friends from church met me for breakfast and prayer time at the hospital. Stephanie was doing just a little better than yesterday. However, when I left to go to the office, I had one of those strange feelings that just can't be explained sometimes.

I called Melanie about 9 a.m. and told her that for some reason all I felt like doing was being at the hospital with Stephanie. I gathered a few things at the office to take down to the hospital with me. About 10:30 a.m. I got an urgent call from Melanie's mother. She said to hurry to the hospital, that Stephanie was having some problems.

I drove as fast as I possibly could to get there. My mind seemed to keep wandering. I felt Stephanie would be gone when I got there. The more these thoughts came into my head, the more I tried to tell myself that everything was going to be OK.

I tried to stay focused on the positive, but my mind was racing ninety to nothing.

For some reason I remembered a story that I heard once about a six-year-old boy. The little boy was visiting his grandpa on his farm. They were walking hand-in-hand through the apple orchard. As they approached one of the apple trees, the little boy spotted a single apple turning red ahead of all the others.

"Look, Grandpa! Look!" he said. "A ripe one." So he talked his grandpa into helping him climb the tree to try and retrieve the prize apple.

As the little boy scooted along the branch, it began to dip lower and lower. "Aren't you afraid to go out on a limb like that?" asked Grandpa.

"Well, yes," replied the little boy. "But that is where the apple is!"

Sometimes fear can keep us from serving our families as we should, and it can also keep us from joyful obedience to God's plan for our lives. Scripture tells us in Isaiah 43:1-2:

But now, thus says the Lord, your Creator, O Jacob, and He who formed you, O Israel, "Do not fear, for I have redeemed you, I have called you by name; you are Mine!"

"When you pass through the waters, I will be with you; and through the rivers, they will not overflow you. When you walk through the fire, you will not be scorched, nor will the flame burn you up."

To have confidence in the power, love, and self-discipline God has given us is to have God's calling for our lives in confidence. When we hang onto the main trunk of the tree, we may never be able to reach the ripest apple. We can never be afraid to go out on a limb, because that is where the reward is!

I pulled up to the front of the building and ran up the stairs to the NICU. I was too late. She had experienced an irregular heartbeat, and just like that she stopped breathing. I was in disbelief. Our little girl, who had seemed to come so far these last few days, was now dead and gone. We could not believe this was happening, not after all that we had been through, and certainly not after the good news we had just gotten last night from the doctor.

Our pastor walked up, and the three of us walked around the corner to the waiting room to sit down for a moment and just be quiet and still, trying to let this sink in. We wondered to ourselves, Is this really happening?

After a few minutes, the hospital's social worker came to ask us if we would step down the hall to a little private room for a few moments. Our pastor and family came with us. After I sat down, a nurse brought my little girl to me. For the very first time, I got the opportunity to hold my baby girl in my arms. All I could do was gently stroke her forehead. I could not take my eyes off her. She was such a beautiful little baby.

She looked so peaceful, just like babies do when they are sleeping—only I knew that Stephanie was not going to wake up. I was not going to be able to one day hear her call for her daddy to come to her side. I was not going to get to see her ride off for the very first time when she got her driver's license. I was not going to see my precious little girl on her prom night all dressed up. I was not going to be able to one day walk her down the aisle on her wedding day. And I was not going to be there for her when she had her own first child. All these thoughts overflowed in my mind.

But I did know that one day after I die and go to heaven, Stephanie will call for me and I will then be able to be by her side!

It is hard for me to describe just how I felt at this time. I couldn't cry a tear. It seemed as though I felt more relief for Stephanie than I did grief for me. None of this seemed real. As long as the last twelve days and nights had been, they now seemed like nothing more than a flash in time. It was like a dream that we were beginning to wake up from, or like some of the roller coaster rides that I have been on. All those peaks and valleys and turns that we went through together, to wind up at the end of the ride with only one thing to do, and that is to just get off and keep on moving.

Melanie and I ended these last twelve days that way. The only thing we could do was to look to Jesus Christ for strength and go on to the next day. To go on with our lives and continue to give God the glory in all that we would be involved in, and believe and trust in Him to make good things come out of this experience in our lives. This is God's will.

That's not to say that things are always going to be easy. There are many times in which we just want to give up, to give into the pressures and demands that the world seems to place on us.

It's during these times, these valleys in our lives, that we can grow in the Lord. By our reading the Bible and praying daily, God will reveal Himself through the Scriptures. After a time of perseverance, He will bring us out of the valley and take us to the peak of the mountain, to where only the cross of Christ shines. It is here where we hope to hear Jesus say to us, as we read in Matthew 25:21, "Well done, good and faithful servant! You have been faithful with a few things; I will put you in charge of many things. Come and share your master's happiness!"

I don't know if anyone on this earth can really understand just how wonderful and beautiful and joyful and awesome heaven is going to be. From the very moment that we give our lives to Jesus Christ as our Lord and Savior, until the very moment that we go to be with Him in heaven, we should be preparing ourselves, dressing ourselves, and shaping our bodies and souls for His return to earth at any moment.

I remember a story told to me a long time ago about a little boy who lived in Denver who was dying of an incurable disease.

This little boy had expressed a desire to see the president of the United States.

A few months later, President Dwight Eisenhower was vacationing in Denver and heard about the wish of this little boy. Early on a Sunday morning, the presidential limousine unexpectedly stopped in front of this little boy's house. The president got out and went to the front door and knocked. The door was opened by the little boy's father, who stood dumbstruck at the sight of the president of the United States, and the realization of his own sloppy appearance in a T-shirt, worn shoes, and a day's growth of beard. The little boy stood behind his father, and neither of them managed to say much as the famous general and president talked for a few moments, shook hands, and departed.

In the days that followed, the little boy's father told many friends about the exciting visit and his own shame in looking like a hobo before the president of the United States.

As Christians, we need to be cleansed and dressed and ready for the calling of Christ. We must be spiritually clean and always ready to spread the gospel to those lost and hurting souls around us, whenever those times may come into our lives.

## Wednesday, June 28

Our little girl, Stephanie Louise Sanford, was laid to rest today. She did so much for so many in the short twelve days that she was with us. She probably did more than many of us could do in a lifetime. I only hope that I can live out the rest of my life in a way she would have been proud of. So that one day, one glorious day, when we meet again and join hands in heaven, she will say that she is proud to be my daughter, because I was the best daddy that I could be.

Stephanie, your mother and I will always love you and will never forget you. I hope that we will both be able to go and tell others of your wonderful life and all the ways in which God has confirmed His presence in your life and in ours.

I wrote a letter to our son, Trey, that night that Melanie and I would give to him when he was older and could understand a little more about what had gone on these last few days. It read:

June 28, 1989
Dear Trey,

Today we put to rest your little baby sister, Stephanie. She was only twelve days old. But, Trey, your sister did more in those twelve days for the cause of Christ than most people will do in a lifetime. She brought many, many people and churches together through the power of prayer and showed many of us what prayer can accomplish when we pray for specific reasons.

Your mother and I took you back to the cemetery after everyone had left and the flowers had been laid over the top of her grave. We told you that she had gone to be with Jesus. You wanted us all to go and get her. We tried to explain, as best we could, that her body was under the flowers but that her spirit is with Jesus in heaven. We wanted you to remember that, and someday you would understand a little more what that meant. This was a very difficult thing for us to talk about with you.

Trey, these last thirteen days have been very hard for you also. Your mother and I have had to spend a lot of time at the hospital with Stephanie, while you were with grandparents, aunts, uncles, and friends. We are real sorry that you had to go through this, but we needed to be at the hospital as much as we could.

I want you to know that we never stopped loving you for one moment and that if we hadn't had you to come home to, we might not have made it through these days.

I hope that as you continue to grow, we can be the kind of parents that God would have us to be and that when you read this letter you might be able to understand a little better what these last thirteen days have been like for us. Even though your little sister has gone on to be with the Lord, she left a lot of good behind and changed a lot of lives, two of those being your mother and father.

May God bless you.

We love you,
Your Daddy

The weeks, months, and even years that have followed have been a time of healing and learning about God and growing spiritually in Him. We are understanding a little more each day why His ways are so much better than ours, if we will only listen to and follow them. God is perfect and we are not. God sees and knows the future and we cannot. God has infinite wisdom while ours is very much limited basically to just what we can see. But that is where the faith part comes in. If we knew what was going to happen in our lives, there would be no need for having faith and trusting in God for strength and guidance. Hebrews 11:1 says, "Now faith is being sure of what we hope for and certain of what we do not see."

It is only when we believe that God will fulfill His promises—even when we don't see those promises materializing as soon as we would like—that we demonstrate true faith.

Sometimes when we are suffering it is really hard to outwardly demonstrate faith. The outside world is watching us to see how we Christians handle adversity. And if the truth were known, we are really hurting inside and may not even know what our next move might be.

In the book of Romans, Paul gives us some insight as to why we go through some of the things that we do. Romans 5:1-5 says,

> Therefore, since we have been justified through faith, we have peace with our God through our Lord Jesus Christ, through whom we have gained access by faith into this grace in which we now stand. And we rejoice in the hope of the glory of God. Not only so, but we also rejoice in our sufferings, because we know that suffering produces perseverance; perseverance, character; and character, hope. And hope does not disappoint us, because God has poured out His love in our hearts by the Holy Spirit, whom He has given us.

This does not say that we are to be happy *because* of our sufferings, but that one day we will be able to rejoice in and through them in the hope of Jesus Christ and what He did for us on the cross.

There is another similar verse in James 1:2-4:

> Consider it pure joy, my brothers, whenever you face trials of many kinds, because you know that the testing

of your faith develops perseverance. Perseverance must finish its work so that you may be mature and complete, not lacking anything.

James is not telling us to pretend to be happy when we face pain, but to have a positive outlook because of what trials can produce in our lives. We need to turn our hardships into times of learning. Tough times can teach us perseverance.

Shortly after the death of our little girl, a very dear friend and member of our church gave us a poem that she had written for us. It speaks so well of the feelings we experienced throughout this time and also tells of God's mercy and grace through times such as these. It is titled "A Parent's Prayer":

> Our Father who art in heaven
> We come to you in prayer
> Commending our daughter Stephanie
> To your tender care.
> We thank you, Father,
> For the joy of her birth
> And for the short, sweet time
> We knew her on this earth.
> We realize, God, that it's not
> Meant for us to know
> Why Stephanie was here so briefly

And then had to go.
We know in our minds
That loved ones have to leave
But it's hard to convince our hearts
When they are bereaved.
We trust in your Word that all things
Work together for good
But, Lord, when we are hurting
That's not easily understood.
We had to bid farewell
Before we hardly said hello
And though we know that she's in heaven
O, God, we miss her so!
There wasn't time to discover
The person she was going to be
And we won't share those special moments
All parents yearn to see.
We didn't want her to stay and suffer
But we wish she could have stayed.
There were so many unsung lullabies
So many games unplayed.
But if Stephanie can't be here
Lying on our breast
We know she's resting in the arms
Of the One who loves her best.

It's comforting to picture her
Safe there on the knee
Of the Blessed One who said,
"Bring the little children to me."
And, Lord, we do thank you
For our precious son.
We pray your continued blessings
On this dear little one.
Make us better parents
May our children see you in us.
Let us be the instruments
That bring them to your trust.
Thank you, Lord, for friends
And family joined in prayer.
It is such a comfort
Knowing that they care.
Thank you for our marriage
And for our love that grows each day.
Help us to nurture that love always
For in Jesus' name we pray.
We're asking for your strength
To go on living as best we can.
We claim your promise that one day
We'll be together—a family again.
May our sorrow not be in vain

May it make us more aware
Of those that hurt around us.
May we comfort. May we share.
Help us to know that when
The sun is shining bright
That Stephanie, too, is basking
In the Son's holy light.
And, Lord, on those stormy days
When showers fall from above
We'll be reminded that she is sheltered
Under the umbrella of your love.
There will be days when we are lonely
Then, Lord, would you please
Send us Stephanie's soft sigh
On the warm, gentle breeze.
One day soon when we're gathered home
And at your throne we kneel
We'll understand when the mysteries of
Your great plan are revealed.
There'll be no pain in heaven
There'll be no sorrow or tears
And this separation will seem like a moment
In the span of eternity's years.

As I said in the beginning, God was always sending us His grace and strengthening us through the calls and letters that we received. There was another poem that a friend sent us just a few weeks after Stephanie died. It was at a time when we were both feeling sorry about her not being able to live out a *full* life, and talking about all those things that she was going to miss out on doing. This poem, titled "A Letter to Mommy & Daddy," held the most comforting words that we could ever have read.

> I just wanted to let you know that I made it home.
> The journey wasn't an easy one, but it didn't take too long.
> Everything is so pretty here, so white, so fresh, and new.
> I wish that you could close your eyes and that you could see it too.
> Please try not to be sad for me.
> Try to understand. God is taking care of me…I'm in the shelter of His hands.
> Here there is no sadness, no sorrow, and no pain.
> Here there is no crying, and I'll never hurt again.
> Here it is so peaceful when all the angels sing.
> I really have to go for now—I've got to try my wings.

The most perfect words sent at the most perfect time. It seems as though God has always continued to shower us with blessings. And just when we thought we were getting dry, He would shower us again. He just wouldn't let us get too low emotionally or in feeling sorry for ourselves.

In fact, for several years Melanie and I led a ministry at our church called In God's Hands, for those who had experienced a miscarriage, stillbirth, or any loss of an infant in the first year of life. (Melanie and I were sort of the "old folks" in the group.)

God has done so much in the lives of our family since that time. I could not possibly begin to tell you all of it. What is so amazing is that God still continues to bless us in ways that we could not have imagined. It is as if Stephanie's story will continue on until we all unite with her in heaven.

There is a scripture in the New Testament that brings it all home for us. It is 2 Corinthians 1:3-5. The apostle Paul writes,

Praise be to the God and Father of our Lord Jesus Christ, the Father of compassion and the God of all comfort, who comforts us in all our troubles, so that we can comfort those in any trouble with the comfort that we ourselves have received from God. For just as the sufferings of Christ flow over into our lives, so also through Christ our comfort overflows.

God knows just exactly how it feels to lose a child. He watched His Son suffer and ultimately die a painful death on a cross. His plan for us is to go to the aid of those who have been through the same trials we have been through. Just as Christ has comforted us, we likewise are to comfort others. This, too, is His continuing plan for our own healing and growth.

Not too long ago, at one of our In God's Hands meetings, some were sharing about how much we miss not having our children to hold in our arms. The strangest feeling came over me that is very difficult to describe, but it could only have been from the Holy Spirit of God. For one very brief moment, God allowed me to see just a little bit of His glory and what He means by "working all things together for good to those who love God, to those who are the called according to His purpose."

I knew that my little girl was experiencing so much more than I ever could have experienced by holding her in my arms. Now that does sound strange, but it is the truth. I knew that she was much better off in God's hands than in mine. That feeling left me just as quickly as it came upon me.

God's wish and desire is to see everyone come to know His Son Jesus in a personal way. Sometimes things happen that we don't understand, but ultimately they can work for the good of God's will in bringing as many people into His kingdom as possible.

What was so special was that God allowed me to see, in that very brief moment, that it was through Stephanie's death, not her life, that more people would come to know Him, and He would have more glory in that. When He gave me that quick glimpse of His plan, I was able to understand a little more. Part of His plan for my life consisted of experiencing the loss of a child. Do I totally understand this and why it happened? No. But do I totally trust in God? Yes.

To those of you who have experienced the loss of a child, a stillbirth, or a miscarriage, let me say to you that even after twenty-four years, God still reigns as Lord of my life. He has always been good and gracious and has always been faithful to His Word and His promises and always will be. God has not forgotten you, nor has He forsaken you at any time, and especially during the time in which you were going through your own personal experience and later grieving the loss of your child.

To those of you who know someone who is going through similar times as these, experiencing some of the same hurdles that we faced, let me encourage you to do the very best thing you possibly could do for that person or family—that is to just *be there for them and with them during these times*. What they need to know is that God loves them, that you love them, and that you are right there if they need to talk about anything or just need a shoulder to cry on.

And to those of you who are even now in the midst of your storm, experiencing the deep anguish of having your child on the edge of life, still in the hospital, and not knowing what the next day will bring, let me offer a bit of comforting advice. Do your very best not to pay attention to all the tubes and instruments that may be hooked up to your son or daughter monitoring their condition for every moment they take a breath. These instruments will surely swing up and down as the minutes, hours, and even days go along. This can take over your mind if you allow it. Try not to look ahead and think about what their condition may or may not be by the end of the day based on what the monitors are currently showing.

Try *only* to be thankful for the moment that you have with your child, and feel blessed to have that moment. Take things just one hour at a time and not one bit more than that. Just cherish the present moments with your spouse (if you are married), and lean on God to take care of the other.

I hope that somehow this book is able to help in some way with a troubled time that you may be experiencing or have experienced in your life. When we speak of comforting and encouraging scriptures in the Bible, I can't help but recall a few verses in the New Testament. In 1 Thessalonians 4:15-18, the apostle Paul writes,

According to the Lord's own word, we tell you that we who are still alive, who are left till the coming of the Lord, will certainly not precede those who have fallen asleep. For the Lord himself will come down from heaven, with a loud command, with the voice of the archangel and with the trumpet call of God, and the dead in Christ will rise first. After that, we who are all still alive and are left will be caught up together with them in the clouds to meet the Lord in the air. And so we will be with the Lord forever. Therefore encourage each other with these words.

These verses tell us that one day we will go to be with the Lord forever. Then we will be united with our family members who have gone on ahead of us. Paul is attempting to comfort us with the promise of the resurrection of Christ, and so we likewise should comfort one another with this great hope.

God will turn our tragedies into triumphs, our poverty into riches, our pain into glory, and our defeat into victory.

*Epilogue*

# MAY GOD BLESS YOU RICHLY WHILE ON THIS EARTH

On Thursday morning, December 11, 2003, I attended my weekly men's Bible study class at our church. We were studying Wayne Grudem's book *Systematic Theology*.

That morning we were studying the sufficiency of God's Word. What we learned is that God's Word to us, the Bible, is absolutely complete with everything that God wanted to reveal to enable us to live our lives as His Son Jesus Christ lived His.

During the class I made the statement, "For the last fourteen years, I have been adding to the story of my daughter's life. From time to time I would hear a special verse of Scripture, or something from a person's testimony would just stand out, and I would go back and add that to her story because I thought it was something that needed to be told and included to help those who have experienced the loss of a child."

Later that morning, at 10:30 a.m., I got a call from my friend Russ Robbins. About a year and a half ago, I called him to see if he would be interested in writing a small piece for me to include in my story. I wanted him to share what God had done in his life during the time of Stephanie's life, and since then as well. It had been a while since we had talked, so I decided to give him a call this past January. And until this morning I had not heard from him.

When he said hello, I knew right away who it was on the phone and knew that this was a divine appointment from the Lord Almighty Himself.

Russ said that he was sorry and embarrassed for taking so long to write something for me. Every time he sat down to write, so much pain and grief came over him as he thought back to those twelve days that he just could never bring himself to get through it.

I was about to pop, wanting to share with him what we had just studied that morning about God's Word being complete, and my story not being complete, and that whatever it was he had written down, it was in God's plan for it to be included in Stephanie's story. And the last thing he needed to do was apologize for being late, because God's timing is always perfect. So I knew whatever it was that Russ had to say, God most definitely wanted it included in the story of my daughter's life.

So I ask you, is God not good? For the two of us to come together on the same morning after a year and a half, with the exact same thoughts, is nothing short of the glory of God.

Russ was always encouraging me with whatever I seemed to have going on, and he was willing to help in any way.

Likewise, I want to encourage you as you go through this very tough time in your life to look to God for strength and guidance.

Philippians 4:13 says, "I can do all things through Christ, who strengthens me."

If you're not involved in a Sunday school class, I encourage you to join one and get close to a few people with whom you can share your deepest thoughts and hurts. If it had not been for my immediate family, my Sunday school class, and my church family, I don't know how Melanie and I could have gotten through this ordeal in our lives. Someone was always there to lift us up at the time in which we needed it the most.

Words will never fill the void that Melanie and I feel sometimes by not having Stephanie in our lives, and not being able to experience her life with us. All those missed birthdays, Easter dresses, that first date, school dances, and, for me, not being able to walk down the aisle one day with my "Daddy's little girl" on my arm.

But as time goes on it gets a little easier year after year to deal with the reality that this was in fact something that happened in our lives, and it was not just a bad dream we were having. And that God's grace is sufficient for us to sustain anything that may happen in our lifetime. Yes, even the loss of a child.

It has been ten years since I closed that last chapter and a total of twenty-four and a half years since that early Thursday morning in June 1989 when sweet Stephanie was born. Wow, to think that she would have been twenty-three years old on her last birthday! I wonder what kind of a young lady she would have become, what her life would have been like, and what kind of dad I would have been to her.

Even with all of those wonderings, I rest in the truth of God's Word that she has been in the arms of Jesus Christ and in *His* presence all this time, and is so much more alive being in heaven with the Father and the Son, reveling in their glory.

Our gracious heavenly Father has continued to bless me and my family so much more than we could ever deserve. He is still faithful to ALL of His promises that He gave to us.

My oldest son, Trey, is now married, and we are tremendously blessed with a wonderful, godly daughter-in-law, Catherine. Trey is taking seminary classes and seeking to preach God's Word from the pulpit wherever He leads. And Catherine just started teaching kindergarten. My other son, Chase graduated college in May and is seeking a career in the FBI.

I think it is just awesome that all three, in some form or other, will be serving others.

My wife is still a very passionate preschool minister at church. As for me, well, I'm having the time of my life teaching the sixth-grade Sunday school class and helping in the nursery and doing all types of ministry and mission projects that I can get my hands on.

God's plan for all our lives over these past years has been so much better than anything we could have tried to do under our own power and abilities. The pain and suffering that we experienced back in June of 1989, with the brief life and death of our daughter, Stephanie, doesn't compare to the joy that has since been revealed to us in our lives through Jesus Christ.

Romans 8:18 says, "I consider that our present sufferings are not worthy of comparing to the glory that will be revealed in us."

We also read in James 1:2–4, "Consider it pure joy whenever you face trials of many kinds, because you know that the testing of your faith develops perseverance. And perseverance must finish its work so that you may be made mature and complete, not lacking anything."

God said that we would not be lacking anything. And we haven't. It's as if Scripture just jumped off the pages of the Bible and we saw God's Word and promises fulfilled in our lives through our obedience and faithfulness to Him.

If you remember, I told you earlier in the story about a passage of Scripture that we wrote on a piece of poster board and taped to the wall of our hospital room. It was Jeremiah 29:11: "For I know the plans that I have for you declares the Lord. Plans to prosper you and not to harm you. Plans to give you a hope and a future."

And He has given us hope. He is our hope.

I have learned over the years that our only hope is in Jesus Christ. It is that very truth that has certainly been confirmed to me countless times over these past twenty-four years, but I also saw the blessings of God in my life when I began to put into action what He goes on to say in verses 12 and 13: "Then you will call upon Me and come and pray to Me and I will listen to you. You will seek Me and find Me when you search for Me with all of your heart."

It is when we seek God with everything we have that we can see and better understand His will for our lives and what our purpose is in His kingdom building. And all of it is His gift of grace to us.

God is, always has been, and always will be in complete control of His creation. In Colossians 1:16-17, we read, "For by Him all things were created: things in heaven and on earth, visible and invisible, whether thrones or powers or rulers or authorities; all things were created by Him and for Him. He is before all things, and in Him, all things hold together."

But if He is in complete control of everything, then why oh why didn't He let my little girl live? Why didn't He make her heart and lungs strong enough so that she could run and play and live life to the fullest? I asked that question time and time again, and maybe you have asked it as well. What is the answer that God gave you? Or are you still waiting on His answer?

All that I can tell you is that God loves each of us more than we could ever imagine. He loves you and He wants you to experience peace and joy and life—abundant life and eternal life.

Well, how do you do that considering the deep valley you have just been through? The Bible says in Romans 5:1, "We have peace with God through our Lord Jesus Christ." In His infinite wisdom and mercy, God sent His Son Jesus Christ to the earth. Romans 11:33 says, "Oh, the depth of the riches of the wisdom and the knowledge of God! How unsearchable His judgments, and His paths beyond tracing out."

First, you need to know that God loves you. "For God so loved the world that He gave His only Son, that whoever believes in Him shall not perish but have eternal life" (John 3:16).

Second, admit that you are a sinner and that sin has a penalty. "For all have sinned and fall short of the glory of God" (Rom. 3:23). And, "For the wages of sin is death, but the gift of God is eternal life in Christ Jesus our Lord" (Rom. 6:23).

Third, acknowledge God's payment for your sin. "But God demonstrates His own love for us in this: while we were still sinners, Christ died for us" (Rom. 5:8).

Fourth, accept Jesus Christ as your Savior and Lord. Through prayer, personally invite Him to come in and be Lord of your life. "If you confess with your mouth, 'Jesus is Lord,' and believe in your heart that God raised Him from the dead, you will be saved" (Rom. 10:9).

Here is a simple prayer:

Dear God, I confess to You that I am a sinner and need Your forgiveness. I know I cannot save myself. I believe Jesus died for my sins. I turn from my sin and invite Jesus to come into my life as Savior and Lord. I give You my life and want to follow You and live for You. In Jesus' name, amen.

Fifth, have assurance that you are saved. The Bible says in Romans 10:13, "Everyone who calls upon the name of the Lord will be saved." And believe what God says in John 10:10: "I have come that you might have life and have life abundantly."

No one said that this is going to be easy. Trying to pick up and go on with life after the devastating loss of a loved one can be a very difficult thing to do. There is much uncertainty about every aspect of life. And we can't do it alone. We don't have to.

God will be with us every step of the way. We just have to take things one day at a time and one step at a time.

We must have trust and faith in our heavenly Father and Him alone, who cares for us more than we ever could imagine, to walk with us and before us as we continue on our wonderful journey of life.

That is my prayer for you and your family—that you too will experience the peace of God as you give Him the praise and the glory through all things that go on in your life, even if that includes the loss of a child.

# Acknowledgments

Where does a first-time writer begin with acknowledging those who were so very important, influential, and encouraging throughout this twenty-four year process?

I must begin with my wife, Melanie, with whom I share my whole life and being. From that very first moment in time when we looked in each other's eyes, realizing that our just-born daughter was very, very sick, to this day as we have shared our walk of life together.

I must also thank my two sons, Trey and Chase, who have taught me so much through the years. They were the best two sons a dad could have. They helped me understand what really mattered in life and what things just weren't that important. They were always appreciative of the things that they had and never complained about not having enough. Many times they let me know that they just wanted their dad to be their dad, and not to try to be anything more than that.

If not for my good friend, John Paul Basham, who thought enough of me and my story to present it to his co-workers and the Publication Board at Morgan James Publishing, this book would have never made it this far.

A big thanks to my editor, Amanda Rooker, for her kindness, patience, and understanding with a rookie writer.

Finally, I thank God for allowing me the privilege of being Stephanie's father. As sweet as heaven will be when I see Jesus for the first time, it is also sweet to know that my little girl will help my Lord and Savior, Jesus Christ, usher me through the Gates of Pearl and onto the Streets of Gold, where we will be together forever and ever.

# About the Author

Bill Sanford is a graduate of Auburn University and the owner of Banner Industrial Construction Company in Alabama. He enjoys hunting, traveling with his family, college football, the outdoors, and teaching 5th and 6th grade students and youth at his church, as well as working with the pre-school kids. In addition to their daughter Stephanie, who passed away in 1989, he and his wife Melanie have two amazing sons, Trey and Chase, and one awesome daughter—in law, Catherine, who was married to Trey in January of 2012. He also enjoys working on all sorts of ministry projects and going on short term mission trips. This is his first book.